A Simplified
Lugbara – English Dictionary

Compiled by
Paul Ongua Iga

Fountain Publishers

Fountain Publishers Ltd
P.O. Box 488
Kampala

© Paul Ongua Iga 1999
First Published 1999

All rights reserved. No part of this publication may be reproduced or transmitted in any form or by any means, without permission in writing from the publisher.

ISBN 9970 02 105 2

Contents

Preface	iv
Acknowledgements	iv
Alphabet	1
Personal pronouns and the verb to be	1
Personal pronouns and the verb to have	1
Parts of speech	1
Conjugation of verbs	2
Lugbara – English	3
Useful phrases	68
Proverbs idioms and similes	69

Preface

This small pocket Lugbara-English Dictionary has been compiled to assist those interested in a deeper understanding of Lugbara, foreigners learning the language, visitors and tourists.

The Lugbara are found in Arua District in north-western Uganda, alternatively known as West Nile. They also extend into neighbouring Congo. the Lugbara also speak other local languages: Lingala and Kiswahili. Their economy revolves around peasant farming and fishing. Most of their values are reflected in their language.

Acknowledgement

I must acknowledge the late Rev. Father A. Maccagnan at one time Parish Priest of Maraca Mission (Arua) for it was his English-Lugbara-Luo Dictionary that inspired me into writing.

I also acknowledge the contribution of the pupils of Cubiri Primary school most especially the Primary Six and Seven of 1993 – 1995.

I want to thank Mr James Tumusiime for encouraging me to complete this book.

I must also thank Mr. Maxwell Adriko of Radio Uganda for his editorial assistance. I would also like to thank the staff of Fountain Publishers for being cooperative, they have been a great help to me.

Paul Ongua Iga
1998

Alphabet

Lugbara has five vowels. The Lugbara alphabet has 24 letters excluding Q and X.
Below are examples on how they are pronounced:
- A - a as in ant
- E - e as in elephant
- I - i as in ink
- O - o as in orange
- U - u as in boot

Personal pronouns and the verb to be

Mai	:	I	I am
Mi-i	:	You	You are
Eri-i	:	He	He is
Eri-i	:	She	She is
Eri-i	:	It	It is
Ama	:	We	We are
Emi	:	You	You are
Eyi	:	They	They are

Personal pronouns and the verb to have

Madri or madri ci: **I have**
Madri or midri ci: **You have**
Eridri or eridri ci: **He has**
Eridri or eridri ci: **She has**
Eridri or eridri ci: **It has**
Amadri or amadri ci: **We have**
Emidri or emidri ci: **You have**
Eyidri or eyidri ci: **They have**

Parts of Speech

The parts of speech in Lugbara grammar are almost the same as those of the English language

Nouns: *ru   Iga*, (personal name)
            ndri (goat)

Pronouns: ma-i (*I*), mii (*you*), eri-i (*he, she, it*)

Verbs: yezu (*to do*), nyazu (*to eat*)
Adjectives: onzi (*bad*), Onduaru (*clever*)
Adverbs: mbelembele (*quickly*), eyere (*slowly*)
Prepositions: ania (*in*), dri (*over*)
Interjections: Oh! (Oh!), ah! (ah!)

Imperatiave: amu-u (*Let us go*), emu (*you go*),
Plural: emuu (*you go*)

Gerund: muu *(going)*, nee *(seeing)*, ojiruu *(bathing)*

Conjugation of verbs

Yesterday	Now	Tomorrow
Ajee amu I went	*Andru ma muu* I am going	*Drusi manga muu* I shall go
Ajee emu You went	*Andru mi muu* You are going	*Drusi minga muu* You will go
Ajee mu He went	*Andru eri muu* He is going	*Drusi eringa muu* He will go
Ajee mu She went	*Andru eri muu* She is going	*Drusi eringa muu* She will go
Ajee mu-u It went	*Andru eri muu* It is going	*Drusi eri nga muu* It will go
Ajece amu-u We went	*Andru ama muu* We are going	*Drusi amanga muu* We shall go
Ajee emu-u You went	*Andru emi muu* You are going	*Drusi eminga mu* You will go
Ajee muu They went	*Andru eyi muu* They are going	*Drusi eyi muu* They will go

Almost all Lubgara verbs are conjugated in the same manner as above.

A
A a *is the first letter of the Lugbara alphabet*

a (ale), stomach, belly, gizzard e.g. in birds)
aa, no, not at all
a a the other side, across e.g. a river
a a (alenia), Inside, within, among
Aba, a mountain in Lugbara land on Zaire side
abaa (abaza), doubting, being confused
abala, competition, betting
abala mbezu, to bet
abalata, a bull
abari, a greater part, the majority
abata, duck
abaza, confusion, doubt
abazu, to doubt, to be confused
abe, handle, a club
abebe, a dumb person
abefe, a bridge
abeleso, a worm, especially in the stomach e.g askaris
abi, wall
abi, grandfather, ancestor
abici, heart - burn
abiri, hunger, famine
abu, a valley
abudira, catapult
abuo, a dove
abua, banana
abuu, covering
abuzu, to cover
acalaka, a trap for fish
acaraka, a trap for fish
acepiri, remainder
acetaa, remaining
acezu, to remain
aci, fire

aci, a journey, travel, safari, trip
acia, on a journey, on safari, on a trip
aciaci, sharp, acute
aci aci, hot
aci aci, share equally
aciandre (aci olu), flame
acife, witchcraft
acika , smoke
aciga , smoke
acikulu, charcoal
aco , a hoe
aco , a fight, a battle
acoo, being lame
acoza , a lame (a person)
acozu, to be lame
ada, true, right, correct, real, genuine
adataa , insult, abuse
adaza, pouring
adaza , week, feeble, spoiled
adazu, to pour
adi, war, battle, fight
adi i?, who?
adii, cooking, boiling
adii, tying
adii, deserting , abandoning
adizu, to cook, to boil
adizu, to desert, to abandon
adizu, to tie
adra , anger
adra , tongue
adraka , poison
adriazi, brother
adrii, brother
adripi , brother
adriza , behaviour, conduct, manners.
Adroo , God, the blessed Trinity, the Father, the Son and the Holy Spirit as opposed to **adrogoa** i.e. evil spirit
adro , maternal uncle

adrogoa , a false god, an idol
adroi , maternal uncle
adromva , nephew, niece
adu?, what?
adu, silver
adukule, alone, in solitude
adungare ya?, when?
adu ni ya? , what is it?
adu si ya? , why?
adu ya? , what?
afa , a thing, something, a being.
afa, riches, wealth, opulence
afa ba , good things
afa da , that thing
afa maa, depreciating, devaluing, underrating, minimizing things
afa mazu, to depreciate, devalue, underrate, minimize things
afazu , utensils
afu , pride, ambition
afuru , proud, ambitious
agaa, passing, being promoted to
agaa , in the middle, between, among, amid
agapia, near, next to beside, in the presence of
agara , exceeding, more than needed
agaraba, a European
agata , protest , dispute, debate
agata gaa, protesting
agata gazu, to protest, to dispute, to debate
agati, chest
agazu, to pass, to go beyond measure, to be promoted to
agbatara, struggle, debate, discussion
ago (anyapa ni), male (for animals)
ago, pumpkin, vegetable marrow
agofe , post, pole
agoliroa , evening star
agu, friend, comrade, companion
agupi , husband, a man as opposed to a woman
agupia (okoni), married (especially for women)

agupia mva, son, lad
Agusto, August, 8th month of the year
ai, answer, response
ai, salt
aifia , salt
aii, affirming, saying "yes"
aii, begging, getting
aii, believing, accepting,
ayiko , happiness, joy, jubilation
airibe, scabbies, itches
airive , scabbies, itches
aitaa, affirmation, saying "yes", accepting, acceptance
aitaa, begging, getting
aitaa, believing, accepting
aizu, to affirm, to say "yes", to accept
aizu, to beg, to get
aizu, to believe, to accept e.g. in religious matters
aja , envy, jeolousy
aje, price, cash
ajee , yesterday
ajeni , the value, the cost - price
ajetaa , marriage, buying
aji, taste, flavour, savour
aji, luck, favouritism
aju , spear, javelin
aju , poles for a house
aka , purposely, deliberately, intentionally
aka , big, great, enormous, grand
akanya , an ass, a tamed animal, an animal of burden e.g. camels, elephants, horses
akaza , soft, tender
ako, without, in vain
aku, home
akua, at home
akuu, covering
akuzu, to cover
ala, clean, smart, neat

alapapa , butterfly
alataa , cleanliness, neatness, smartness
alaza (tibi ni), cooked with condiments (for vegetables)
alaza , put across
ale, stomach, belly
ale , love, liking
alea , inside, in the stomach, in the gizzard (for birds)
ali, deep
ali, crime
ali, a part of the dowry, bride-price paid for a bride
alia , short
alibaa , committing adultery, committing fornication
alibazu, to commit adultery, to commit fornication
alibo , partridge
alii, cutting
alimva, bastard, an illegal child
alio , poverty
alio , poor
alioru , poor
aliria , virgin
alizu , to cut
alizu , to menstruate
alo , a peg for tethering a goat
alo alo , loose, not tight
alo ani yo!, not at all!
aloo, loose
alofe, bridge
alozori, the first, prime
alozu, to be loose
alu , red cat
alu , one
alu alu , one by one, singly
alugbe, an unhatched egg
alu toko, only one
aluza, sweet, palatable
aluzaru, sweet, palatable
ama , we
amamu, pigeon

amangingi, mumps
amataa, assessment, judgement
amazu, to assess, to judge
amba, ambush
amba, preambulator, pram
ambiza, cold, cool
amboo, master, boss, superior
amuroo, bride, newly wed partner
amvaa, mating (for animals)
amvazu, to mate
amve, outside, abroad overseas
amvii, touching
amvii, sister
amvizu, to touch, to get hold of
amvu, garden, field
amvu fazu, to prepare a garden for sowing seeds
amvu yazu, to cultivate, to dig, to till the soil
amvuu, embracing
amvuzu, to embrace
ana/ ano, weed, thistles
ande, tiredness, fatigue
andraa, three days ago, the day before yeasterday
andraleba, the Lugbara in the east, the easterners
andrali, dew
andrapuru, aunt
andre, tongue
andre, mother
andrii, visiting
andrizu, to visit
andru, today
andru, an abandoned home, a deserted village angu, the earth
angu biza, night, darkness
angu dali, valley
angu ndriza   , peace
angu sara, day break
anguturu, beads
ania, inside, within, in

ani beni, in order that, so that
anya, millet
anyabada, omnivorous
anyafura, flour
anyakijo, stomach, belly, gizzard(inbirds)
anyajo, stomach, belly, gizzard (in birds
anyapa, animals
anyapa, dowry, bride-price
anyapa ongulumuru, a herd of animals
anyawio, Adam's apple
anyi, pride
anyi, irony
anyikia, an evil spirit which is supposed to be living in mount Aba
anyiru, proud
anyiru, ironical
anyu, bees
anyu, simsim
anyuoso, honey
anza, penis
anzi, children
anzi nyiri, small children
anzoroko, chain
apaa, running, escaping
aparaka, frivolity, carelessness
aparakaru, frivolous, careless
apataa, running, escaping
apazu, to run away, to escape
ape, exchange of animals with animals that are in calf
apereti, dung-hill, surrounding near the home
apii, getting satisfied, satiated
apinaka, hedge-hog
apipia, abscess, boil
apizaru, satisfied, satiated
apizu, to get satisfied, to satiate
apizu, to break into pieces
ara, python
araa de , around here

ari, blood
ari, drum
aria, bird
ariboo, enemy, adversary, rival
ari adaa, shedding blood
ari coo, drumming
aricozu , to drum
arika, dysentery
arika suu, diarrhoea
arioti, revenge, vengeance, tit-for-tat
arioti ofezu, to take revenge, to revenge
aro , eight
aro, medicine
arojo , hospital, dispensary, clinic, drug-shop
arozori, the eighth
aru, slave, prisoner
Arube , an imaginary ancestor of the Lugbara people who lived many years ago and whose wife was said to have been called Oduu
asalaa , among, between, within
asara , loss in business (derived from swahili)
ase , grass
asea, in the bush, outside the country
asi , heart
asi driasi, willingly, whole-heartedly
asi duzu , to worry, to bother, to be preoccupied
asi duzu te, not to pay attention to
asii, ending, finishing, completing
asiliza , stomach ache, stomach trouble
asi ndriza, mercy, mercifulness
asi onzi, malice
asi onziru, malicious
asi otiza, worry, preoccupation
asisi, willingly, on one's own accord, whole heartedly
asisile , reason, opinion, the quidity
asi teza, patience, tolerance, endurance
asizu , to end, to finish, to complete
asizu, to tear.
asizu, to split

asu, persuasion
asu suzo , to persuade
ata , father
ata, by all means
atapuru, paternal uncle
atete, swamp
atiboo, servant
atii, curing, healing
atii, supporting, siding with
atii, father
atii, getting drunk, getting intoxicated
atizu, to cure, to heal
atizu, to support, to side with
atizu, to get drunk, to get intoxicated
atuluku, fire-place, stove, cooker
atua, squatting
atoloo, sir, Mr. Esq.
atuzu, to squat
au, chicken, hen
au andrii, a hen
au ata, a cock
au ata ceresi, at cock crow
au mvaa, a chick, a pullet
auu, yawning
auzu, to yawn
ava, breath
avaliza, rest
avalizu, to rest
avataa, desiring, coveting
avataa, coveting (desire)
avataza, covetousness (desire)
avatazu, to covet, to desire
avii, losing
avii, playing
avivi, steam
avivi, scent, smell , flavour, stinking smell
avizu, to lose
avizu, to play

avuu, boiling, cooking
avuzu, to boil, to cook
awa, quarrel
awaa, dividing
awadifo, thanks
awadifo yoo, thanking, being grateful to
awadifo yozu, to thank, to be grateful to
awata, raw, unripe
awataa , division
awataa, quarreling
awazu, to quarrel
awazu, to divide, to share among
awete di! , there you are!
awhi, dry
awi, concupiscence of the flesh, sting of the flesh
awio, sexy, a sexy person
awii, remaining
awita, heritage
awita nyaa, inheriting
awita nyazu , to inherit
awizu, to remain

B

B b *is the 2nd letter of the lugbara alphabet*

ba , human being
ba, breast
ba, o.k. good, alright
baa, putting
ba acoza, a lame person
ba acozaru, a lame person
ba acuu, mistreating, malicing
ba aka, a big man
ba ako, without any relative, lonely
ba akua, villager, native
ba ala, a good man, a holy man
ba asalaa, among us, within us

ba azaza, a lunatic, a mad man
ba aza koo, helping people
ba aza kozu, to help people
ba azi, somebody
ba aziyo, nobody, none
baba, good, right, just, o.k
Baba, a child's name for his father
baci, there is somebody
bacii, biting a person with the teeth
ba cizu, to bite a person with the teeth
ba daa, insulting a person
badabada, disorderly, at random
badakaru, a great quantity
ba dazu, to insult a person
badaa, insulting a person
ba deza, an old person
ba dezu, to curse a person
ba gaa, denying a person
ba gazu, to deny a person
ba guu, laughing at a person
ba guzu, to laugh at a person
ba ii, imprisoning
ba izu, to imprison
baka, rope
bako, without relatives
bakule, bowl
balangiti, blanket
balandiki, blanket
bamia, lady finger
bamuu, let us go
bana, three people
bandre, queen, lady
bandu, a different person
ba nguu, hating people
ba pililiru, a naked person
ba piri, all people
ba piri, a straight-forward man, a just man, the right man
bari, at our home

baasa, envelope
basala, onions
basi?, how many people?
batania, blanket
bati, corrugated iron sheets
bati, curse
batrego, a person who does not do his or her work smartly esp women who do not cook palatable food, dirty.
bau, board, wood
bayo, nobody
bazu, to put
be, mountain
be, with
bee, throwing
bee, laying (e.g. eggs or bricks)
bee, pouring a portion of liquid
bele, of course, obviously
bele, wound
bendere, flag
bendere ii, hoisting a flag
bendere izu, to hoist a flag
beseni, basin
bezu, to lay eggs or bricks
bezu, to throw
bezu, to pour a portion of liquid
bi, ear
bi, hair
bibi, dark
bibia, bat
bibia, umbrella
bibio, star
bido, jeerycan
bii, darkening, becoming dirty
bii, mudding a house
bii, tasting
bii, arresting, getting hold of
biko, hair
biko, feather

14

bile, hole
bile, wound
bile , ear
bileko, a deaf person
bilendu lii, warning
bilendu lizu, to warn
bili , chair
binika , teapot, tea kettle
bizaru, dark, black, dirty
bizu, to dirt
bizu, to mud a house
bizu, to arrest, to get hold of
bo!, you see!
bodi di , you see!
bolo , chicken roost
bongo , clothes
bonyo, axe
boroko, a temporary hut, cottage
boroo, insects
buroo, somebody, an alien, stranger, foreigner.
bu, sky, heavens
bu, heaven
bua , in the sky, in the heavens
bua , in heaven
hualeru, towards the sky, towards the heavens
bualeru, towards heaven
buku, book
bunia , fist
bura , cat
buroo , an alien, stranger
buru, at home
burugo , insects
burusu, cow peas
buruu , regret
buruu aizu, to regret
busu, cat
buzaru, covered
buzu , to cover

C

C c *is the 3rd letter of the Lugbara alphabet*

caa , reaching
caa , cackling (e.g. of a chicken)
caa , becoming wet as a result of fermentation
caa , knitting, weaving, plaiting e.g. hair
cabo, enough, sufficient
cai , tea
candi, trouble, suffering, danger
candiru , troublesome, causing suffering, dangerous
capirisi, just enough
cara, enough
carani, sewing machine
cataa , arrival
cazu , to reach
cazu, to cackle
cazu, to become wet as a result of fermentation
cazu, to knit, to weave
cazu pere, u p to, to reach up to the limit or destination
ceni, by itself, automatic
cere, yell
cere bezu, to yell (e.g to indicate somebody is dead)
ci , present
cii, masticating
cii , mating (for chickens)
cinya , sand
cinyafi, sand
cinyaki, sand
cizu , to masticate, to bite
cizu , to mate
colokpoa, a horn used for keeping gum for trapping birds for food.
coo , beating, caning, flogging
coo , weaving (e.g. a granary)
coo , tapping termites
coo , sneezing
coroni, excrement, faeces, waste matter)

coroni, latrine
coroni baa, defecating
coroni bazu, to defecate
coroni bile, latrine - pit
coroni tezu, to break wind
coti , at once
cozu , to beat, to cane, to flog
cozu, to weave, (e.g. a granary)
cozu , to tap termites
cozu, to sneeze
cua, weaver bird
cucurudo, just now
culu, heart
culu ni caa , heart beat
cupa, bottle
curudo , now
cuu , market

D
D d *is the 4th letter of the Lugbara alphabet*

da , there
daa, there
daa, kissing
daa , fasting, abstaining from food for religious reason
daa , insulting a person
daa , pouring a liquid
dale , in that direction
daleru , in that direction
dani , like that
dani , may be, perhaps
danidani, everlasting
daru te , getting away
daruzu te, to get away from
dawa , medicine, drugs
dazu, to kiss
dazu, to fast, to abstain from food
dazu, to insult

dazu, to pour
de , here
dede, grand mother
dee , falling
dee, breathing the last breath before death, dying
dee , becoming old
Decemba , December, the 12th month of the year
deko, not at all
dele, there, in that direction
deleru, towards there, in that direction
deni, debt
deno , debt
derisa, window
derubo, finished
deza , old
dezu, to fall
dezu, to become old
dezu, to finish
di , this
dia , here
dii , this one
dii, killing
dii , pounding
dii, shining *dii ,* getting fed up, getting tired
dika , again
dika ku, never again
dini, like this
dinile , like this
dini yo, not like this
dipi, this much, enough
dirisa, window
dizu, to kill
dizu, to pound
dizu, to shine
dizu, to get fed up with, to get tired of
do, here
doa, here
doi, this one near me

dokani, unless
dole, towards here, to me
doru , keeping silent, being taciturn
doruzu , to keep silent, to be taciturn
dra, death
draa, dying
draa, at a funeral ceremony
draa, a smoking pipe
draa, sour, bitter
dradra, sour, bitter
dra okangali, it is very sour or bitter
dranga , a smoking pipe
drara , is dead
draza, sour, bitter
draza, a dead one
drazu, to be sour or bitter
drazu, to die
dri, hand
dri, head
dri, to
dria, all
dria, on the head, above, over
dria dria, all, every
driada , right hand
dri ago, tumb
dri anzi, fingers
dria avi, forgetfulness
driavi si, due to forgetfulness
driaviza , forgetfulness
dribi, hair
dribifu, grey hair
drifuu, meeting somebody
drigaza, headache
drii , hot
drilea , in front, before
drileba, fortune, luck
drilejo , index
drileji, left hand
drileonzi, misfortune, bad luck

drinia , on it, on top of it
drimvaa, finger
drinza , shame, disgrace
drinzaru, shameful, disgraceful
drisi, by hand
drisi, by heart
drisi, on the head
drio , long ago, once
driokpo, stubbornness, obstinacy
driondi, litterally, dirty hands
driondi, poison
drionzi, stubbornness, obstinancy
drionziru, stubborn, obstinate
dririma , punishment
drizaru, hot, warm
drizu , to be hot , to heat
drozi, the day after tomorrow
dru, tomorrow
dru dru, daily, always
drusi, tomorrow
du, sudden, unexpected
dufara, fermented millet or maize used for   making
        beer
duku, hiccup
dulua , short
duluamva, a dwarf, a short person
duluaru , short
dununu , smooth, tender, nice to touch (e.g. of the skin)
duu , taking
duu , igniting, setting on fire, burning
duu , belching
duzu, to take
duzu , to ignite, to set on fire, to burn
duzu , to belch

E

E e *is th 5th letter of the Lugbara alphabet*
ebede, tea without sugar

ebi, fish
ebi, fresh, uncooked
Ebi, a river in Lubgara land in Haut Zaire
ebile, wound
ebibi, leaves
ebii, gumming, sticking with gum
ebizu, to gum, to stick with gum
ebu, a hoe
ebusi, a valley
ecaa, arrival, arriving, reaching
ecaa, white ant
ecandii, molesting, troubling
ecandizu, to molest, to trouble
ecazu, to arrive at, to reach
ecee, showing, demonstrating, explaining
ecezu, to arrive at, to reach
ecee, showing, demonstrating, explaining
ecezu, to show, to demonstrate, to explain
ecii, deceiving, delaying, locking, joining
ecizu, to deceive, to delay, to lock, to join
ecoo, being able, being capable of
ecozu, to be able to, to be capable of
eda, picture, photo, statue
edataa, showing, demonstrating
edazu, to show, to demonstrate
edee, falling
edee, making fool of
edee, making, doing, acting
edezu, to fall
edezu, to make fool of
edezu, to make, to do, to act
edetaa, foolery
edra, mother-in-law
edri, life
edri, healthy, strong
edrii, mother-in-law
edrika, mushroom
edriru, alive

21

edoo, beginning, commencing, starting, initiating
edotaa, beginning, starting,, commencing, initiating
edoza, beginning , starting
edozu, to begin, to start, to commence, to initiate
edroo, a rat
ee , yes
efee, giving (towards) the speaker)
efezu, to give (towards) the speaker)
efi , seed
efi , meaning
efi , need, neccessity, meaning, result
efitaa , entrance
efi yaa , to have meaning, to produce result
efikoko, meaningless, needless
efutaa, exit
egaa, resurrecting, rising from death
egaa , remembering recalling
egaraka, a crab
egazu, to resurrect, to rise
egazu, to remember, to recall
egbe, cold, coldness
egbee , becoming cold
egbeeru, cold
egbezu, to become cold
egbezu , to bark (of a dog)
eja , firewood
eje , a rib
ejii, bringing
ejiizu , to bring
eju , twins
ejuu, stretching
ejuzu, to stretch
eka , red
ekaru , red
eka , sugarcane
eka, if
ekaa, helping
ekazu, to help

ekele, cough
ekele gazu, to cough
eklesia, church
elee, deceiving
elee, changing position
elekendre, chameleon
eleu, testicles
elezu, to deceive
elezu, to change position
eli, year
eli, lust, desire for something
eli, knife
elifu alo , one thousand
elifura, dust
elii, tickling
elio , fig tree
elizu , to tickle
emaa, owl
emaa, manuring a place
eliriga, millipede
emazu, to manure a place
emba, moon, month
embazu, to learn, to teach
emba, fishnet
embaa , learning, teaching
embapi, a teacher
embataa, teaching, doctrine
emgbilia , trap for animals
emi , you (Plural)
emgbeleke, chimpanzee, a species of ape
emutaa, adding, summing up
emuu, adding, summing up
emuzu, to come
emutaa, coming
emuzu, to add, to sum up
enaa, bewitching
enataa, bewitching
enazu, to bewitch

endra, meanness
endra ako, generous
endra ako, generosity
endrao, a mean person
endrika, shade
endrilendri, shadow
endu, buttocks
endu, anus
endundaa, undermining
endundazu, to undermine
engaa, originating, deriving from, waking up, germinating
engazu, to originate, to derive from, to wake up, to germinate
engo, song, hymn, carrol
engo ngoo, singing
engo ngozu, to sing a song, a hymn, a carrol
eni, snake, serpent - any type of snake
eni, skin,
eniriko, skin,
emvu, pot
emvua, orphan
emve, white
emvua, pot - (a small pot)
enya, cooked millet baked food
enyataa, poison
enyakinya, poison
enyi, hides
enyi, near
enyiriko, hides
enyia, near
enza, laziness, indolence, idleness
enzaa, maltreating
enzamatara, mistreatment
enzaru, lazy, indolent
enzo, a lie
enzoba, a lier
enzo lii, telling a lie
enzo lizu, to tell a lie, to kid
epitaa, exaltation

epizu, to exalt, to praise oneself or somebody
era , granary
ere , far
eree, spreading
erezu, to spread
erifura, dust
eri i , he, she, it
eriti , for good, forever
erii , hearing, listening, understanding
erizu, to hear, to listen, to understand
ero , granary
ero , medicine
ero coo, making a grannary
ero cozu, to make a granary
ese, grasshopper
esele, border, demarcation line
ese ruu, catching grasshopper for food.
ese ruzu, to catch grasshoppers
esuu, finding
esu, vein, tendon
esuzu , to find
etaa , tempting, testing
etataa, temptation, test
etata, rain -water, puddles
etatangule, tad pole
etazu , to tempt, to test
Eti, the highest mountain in Lugbara land
eti , tamarind
eti, buttocks
etiriko, snail
etirili, cricket
etoo, hare, rabbit
etoo, saving , redeeming
etopi, saviour, redeemer
etozu, to save, to redeem
etu , sun
etu , borassus tree
etusi, during the day

etu alasi, in the evening
etu diti (Etuzu), the whole day
etu siya?, what time is it?
etu ni iombe nyoria, in the afternoon
etu ni deria, at sun-set
etu sile, the sun heat
evee, burning
evezu, to burn
evoa, basket (a small one)
ewa, beer,
ewa, an elephant
ewa, power
ewadri, tust
ewapa, elephantiasis
ewaru, difficult
ewasi, ivory
ewii, trapping
ewii, making accustomed, getting used to
ewizu, to trap
ewizu, to make accustomed, to make used to
eyi, they
eyio, crocodile
eyi siya?, How many are they?
eyo, a word, saying, matter
eyo erizu, to obey
eyo lii, judging
eyo lipirii, judge
eyo lizu, to judge
eyo ma ti pezu, to inform
eyo ngonia, How are you? What is the matter?
eyo nzee, speaking, talking
eyo nzezu, to speak, to talk
Eyo yo, very well, no problem
eza, meat
eza, sin
ezaa, sinning, spoiling, mistaking
eza gaa, repenting
ezagazu, to repent

ezazu , to sin; to spoil things
eze , dung, faeces, waste matter
eze tee , gassing, breaking wind
eze tezu, to break wind, to gas
eze zee, defecating
eze zezu , to deficate, to ease oneself, to empty one's bowels
ezi, long
ezii , praying
ezitaa , prayer
ezizu, to pray
ezo , fiance
ezo azii, courting
ezo azizu, to court
ezu , long
ezoo aseari, worthog
ezoo, pig
ezuu, multiplying, increasing
ezuru, long
ezuzu, to multiply, to increase
egoa, small axe
eyere eyere, slowly slowly
egoo, returning, coming back
egozu, to return, to come back
etu ni ekaa, the sun is rising
etu ni ekazu, for the sun to rise
eboroje, antelope
ezutaa, multiplying, increasing
ezoo, bringing up
ezozu, to bring up.
ewani yo, easy, not difficult
ezu , long
ewakokoru, easy, not difficult, weak, feeble
endiria, duicker

F

F f *is the 6th letter of the Lugbara alphabet*
faa , cutting hair with a razor blade

fala , bone
falako, bone
farasi, horse
fe , tree
Februali, February, the 2nd month of the year
fee , giving
feremu, frame
fetaa, gift, present, fund-raising
fezu, to give, to present, to fundraise
fi , intestine
fi (si), hail stone
fi gbuliujo , large intestine
fii , entering
fii , becoming cold (ambiza)
fitina , grudge (Kiswahili language) meaning (asi onzi)
fizu , to enter
fizu , to become cold (egbe ru)
foloko, bones
foo , itching
forojilo, pale
foro , grey
forotolo, brother (religious person)
foro , tilapia (fish)
fozu , to itch
fu, flower
fungua , key
funo, groundnuts
fura , in the state of flour, or dust
fukufuku, bellows
furufuru , lung
fundru, flour
fuu, fighting
fuu, going out
fuzu, to fight, to wrestle, to combat
fuzu, to get out
fifi, cold

G

G g *is the 7th letter of Lugbara alphabet*
gaa, cutting, felling down a tree
gaa, refusing, denying
gaa, creeping, crawling
gaagaa, crow
gadigadi, coach, wheel-barrow
gakinyaa, very small, very little
galaba, snake, serpent (a type)
galawuri, lamp-glass
gari, bicycle
gari, rain-bow
garimosi, train
gataa, refusal, denial, negation
gazu, to refuse, to deny, to negate
gbaa, beating, caning, hitting, kicking the ball
gbanda, cassava
gbazu, to kick a ball
gbazu, to beat, to cane, to hit
gbe, egg, ovum
gbe oboko, shell
gbee, vomiting
gbezu, to vomit
gbii, shooting
gbiniki, habitat
gbizu, to shoot
gbolo, bed, wood used to sleep on in the olden days
gboro, Adam's apple
gbudri, shoulders
gerema, branch
geri, way, path, lane, track
geriko, way
gobolo, lice, louse
godogodo, crocked
golo, football
golo tuzu, to play football
gunga, trumpet
gunia, sack

gurunya, yam
guru , deep
guu , laughing, laughter
guu , pushing down
gutaa , laughter, laughing
guzu , to laugh, to jeer at
guzu mgbu, to push down

H

H, h *is the 8th letter of the Lugbara alphabet*
hahaa!, an expression of laughter
hai!, an expression of surprise in denial or in affirmation (affirmative)
hau, an expression used when burnt suddenly , or to cut deep or big
hii , an expression of surprise in regrets
hehee! , an expression of laughter

I

I, i *is the 9th letter of the Lugbara alphabet*
ibi , raw, uncooked, immature
ibi , fish
ibio , spider
ibiru, raw, uncooked, immature
icikici, black stinging ants
icii, deceiving
icitaa, deceit
icizu, to deceive
ii , imprisoning
ii , grinding
ili, knife
ini , snake, serpent (only a type)
ini , night
ini , blackness, darkness
inibilicici, very dark, very black (inibirici)
inii , cleaning, rubbing off, erasing, smearing with
inikurukuru, very black, very dark
iniriko, skin, hides

inizu, to clean, to rub off, to erase, to smear with
iniru, black, dark
imve, white
imve, light, brightness}
imvero , white, bright   } (These start with letter "e" or "i")
imve sirili, very white   }
Inzi, respect, honour, glory
inziru, respectful, polite
inzii, respecting, honouring, glorifying
inzizu, to respect, to honour, to glorify, to worship
iritro, both
iri, two
iri-iri, two by two
iribi, pasture
irifia , wasp
irii, getting fed up with
iriko, broken or torn especially because old, e.g. clothes, utensils
irikoko , very smelly, stinking
iriti, clouds
irizu , to get fed up with
irizuri , the second
iyi , water
iyi agogofi, wave
iyiti, at the shore, at the bank of a river etc.
Izii , praying
izimicicio, I salute you
izimicicio, parrot, sound made by a parrot
izitaa , prayer
izizu , to pray
izu , to grind
izu , to imprison
iga , in prison
idria , razor blade
idrii, mother-in-law
irii , compound, court yard
inziko , without respect, impolite, rude

J

J j *is the 10th letter of the Lugbara alphabet*
jaa, getting cured, healing

jaa, changing position
Jakimirinya, The great grandfather of the Lugbara people
jarara, buttons
jazu, to get cured, to heal
jazu, to change position
jebe, pocket
jee, buying, marrying
jeleko, horn used as a trumpet
jereko, bush
jetaa, buying, marriage
jezu, to buy
jezu, to marry
jii, carrying
jii, becoming pale of cold (body)
jijima, shoes (kiswahili word)
jitaa, carrying
jitaa, becoming plale of cold (body)
jizu, to carry
jizu, to become pale of cold
jo, house, hut, cottage
joa, inside the, in the hut, in the cottage
karia, bicycle
karia, roof
jodri, on the roof
joloko, the remainder
jokoni, kitchen
jokoni, market (sokoni) - Kiswahili word)
jomile, window
jobileko, verandah
jorovu, nest
jotile, door
Julai, July
junya, gigger, sand fly
June, June
juru, behive
juru, foreigner, alien, stranger
juru, big, great, grand
jurua, in the tool - kit!

K

K k *is the 11th letter of the Lugbara alphabet*
kaaka!, an expression of exclaiming!
kaati, door, gate
kabilo, sheep
kabilo ago, ram
kabilo aroni, ewe
kafua, a short used hoe
kafiri, pagan
kafuto, lather, foam
kai, in vain
kaiko, beans
kajoa, calf
kaka, maize
kakau, many, numerous
kala, side
kalaa, metal basin (kalaya)
kalamu, pen, pencil
kalangira, sieve
keyikeyi, sieve
kalasi, aside
kalanya, beef
Kalati, end
kali, stick
kalikali, sweet
kalitusi, eucalyptus tree
kamee, spoon
kami, lion
kana, without
kandi, football, rubber
kania-ni!, may be
kani, may be
kani,if, on condition
kanisi,rather
kanisa, a protestant church
kanita tro, even if, although
kaoo, first

kapia, stork
kapure, tuft
karakara, many, numerous
karakararu, many, numerous
karamoja, a variety of potato vines
karani, clerk
karatasi, paper
kokobi, paper, letter
karile, juvenile, youngster
karii, a young female of an animal e.g. cow, goat etc.
kata , ashes filtered into a liquid form used instead of salt in the olden days (even up to now for cooking source greens)
katara , shoes, boots, galoshes
kau, house
kawa, coffee
kaa , shining
kazu, to shine e.g . sun, moon, stars
keelo, an ass
kelele, disturbance (kiswahili word)
kelele, hot e.g. boiling water
kere, gourd
keyekeye , sieve
kii , swallowing
kalafe, number
kijiko, spoon
kilijiku, a species of cactus tree
kinga , bicycle
kinoo, mortar
kinoo abe, pestle
kitanda, bed
kitambala, handkerchief
kiteyiteyi, frock
kitiyo, spade
kizu, to swallow
ko?, is it?
ku, no, not at all
kodra, papyrus, papyrus mat
kofia, hat, cap, beret

kojaa, calf
koko, firm, tight
kokoa, wood pecker
kokosi, pins, safety pin
kolikoli, wag-tail
kolokolo, loose, not tight
kome , chair
koono, harrow
kopo, cup
kopolo, lock
kori, a kind of fox
korogbolo, very thin, and bony
koosi, (dani toko) purposely, deliberately, intentionally
kpete, local beer,
kpi, straight
kpikpi, straight
kujura, wall partition in a room
kuliabantu, cannibal (a word in Bantu language)
kulu, insects
kulukulu, turkey
kuu, forgiving, giving up -
kuzu, to forgive, to give up
kumu , knee
kumu, stumbling block
kumu sii, kneeling , genuflecting
kumu sii, stumbling at e.g. a stone
kumu sizu, to kneel, to genuflect
kumu sizu, to stumble at
kesi, case
kukuti , the bank of a river
kuku ti, arm pit
kauu , first
kaa ka, an expression of surprise or admiration at seeing something great
kokoo , anything for teasing a kid
kurunya, rubbish
koci koci, all, completely
kali iri, twenty

kali na, thirty
kali su, forty
kali tau, fifty
kali azia, sixty etc.

L

L l *is the 12th letter of the Lugbara alphabet*
laru, banyan tree
lataa, reading
lataa, counting
lataa, sleeping
lazu, to read
lazu, to count
lazu, to sleep
le, milk
le, must, ought, it is obligatory, it is imperative
lee, liking, loving
lejo, index
leleo, morning star
leleri, the beloved one
lelero, the beloved one
lesu, milk
letaa, love, liking
lezu, to love, to like
lico, kraal, cow-shed
lico, home
ligaliga, dragon-fly
likico, orphan
limbo, a state of the human soul after death
lojima, a desert plant
loki, sperm
lokira, elbow
lokiri, trick
lokiriru, tricky
londre, colobus
loo, slaughtering, cutting the ears of corn
loozu, to harvest from the garden or field -(cereals)

loodo, an incurable wound many times causing the amputation of a limb e.g. leg
lozu, to slaughter, (e.g of an animal)
likiti, pocket
litaa (eyo), sentence
Lugbara , the people or language of the Lugbara land
loma , rib
luru , mist, fog
lururu, misty, foggy
lurua , narrow
lulu, alarm
lulu gaa, alarming
lulu gazu, to alarm
laa , counting
laa, reading
laa, lying down
lii, cutting
libibiri, dragon fly
lii, rolling
lii, cleaning (e.g. with water and cloth)
lizu, to cut
lizu, to roll
lizu , to clean
lobeke, spotted

M

M m *is the 13th letter of the Lugbara allphabet*
maa, depreciating, devaluing
maa, rotting, decaying
macira,, tick
madala, ladder
madri , to me
madri i, mine
mafuta , kerosene, paraffin (Kiswahili word)
mai, I
makasi,a pair of scissors
makata, a case
maku, potato

malaga, spoon
malaika, an angel
malaja, slander
malaya, a harlot, prostitute = (a kiswahili word)
mama, a child's name for his mother
mandalina, tangerine
mandili, handkerchief
mani, mine
manjaka, guine-worm
mamva , my child = (ma-mva)
manya, alligator, monitor,
maraa , looking glass, mirror, spectacles
mari, debt
Maria, the blessed Virgin Mary, mother of our Lord Jesus Christ
Marci, march
mariti, penance, punishment
matata, quarrel, disturbance - (a Kiswahili word)
matu, misery, sadness, sorrow
mawua, flower
Mayi, May
mayala, slander
maye!, dear me, my goodness!
mazii, my daughter
mbata, duck
mbaza, an old man
mbazao, an old man
mbii, fucking, playing sex
mbizu, to fuck, to play sex
mbeta, ring
mari, at my home
mbozoo, an old man - (an elderly man)
mbuu, jumping
mbuzu, to jump
mee, a cry of a goat
meja , table
menemene, soft, tender
meu, an expression used for an instant burn
mi , you

midrii, yours
mii, you - (mi-i)
mile, eye
mile aci, curiosity
mile ako, a blindman
mile bi, eye lash
mile fi, eye ball
mile ini , gloominess
milemba , wisdom, cleverness, intelligence
mile ogoliro, squint - eyed
mile ti, face
mindre, tears
mini, yours
milioni, one million
miri, at your home
miri, a big river, lake, sea, Nile
miriko , scar
miru, your name
muke , good, well, o.k
muketu, very good, very well
mokoto, judge
mombe, mangoes
monio , a bull
moskiti, mosque
mucele, rice
mucungua, oranges (a kiswahili word)
mude , darkness
mudri, ten, 10
mufalisi, mattress
mugati, bread
mupira, ball, football
musalaba, cross
musara, salary
musara nyaa , earning salary
musara nyazu, to earn salary
musipi, belt
musoro, tax
musoro bee, paying taxes

musoro bezu, to pay taxes
musumari, nails
mutere, cassava or potato cut into chips and dried for food
mutufali, bricks
mutufali bee, laying bricks
mulufali bezu, to lay bricks
mari, a musical instrument blown in dances
mari fee, paying debts
mariti ofee, doing penance
mari ofezu, to pay debts
mariti ofezu, to do penance
mayembe, a revenging evil spirit in Buganda
mva, child, boy
mamva , my child, my son
mva nii, carrying a baby at the back
mva nizu, to carry a baby at the back
ma adrii, my brother
maru , mushroom
ma amvii, my sister
musumeni, saw
matuuru, miserable, sad, sorrowful
mbelembele, quickly, in a speedy manner
mokoto libo, a final judgement
mileko, a blind man
mile cwiru, bad eyed
maatii, my father
muu, going, departing
muzu , to go , to depart,
muu doria, go hunting
muzu doria, to go hunting
mbuu, jumping
mbuzu, to jump
mbaa, becoming mature
mbazu, to become mature
mvuu, drinking
mvuzu, to drink
mvuu, jumping
mvuzu, to jump

mbaa, laying ambush
mbazu, to lay ambush
Mva, A child
mva ni fuu, miscarrying
mva ni fuzu, to miscarry
mva ofuu, aborting, abortion
mva ofuzu, to abort
mva osii, delivery, delivering
mva osizu, to deliver, to give birth
mva tii, producing a child, bearing a child
mva tizu, to produce a child, to bear a child

N

N, n *is the 14th letter of the Lugbara alphabet*
na, three
naa, dodging
na na, three by three
nana, also, as well, too
nanasi, pineapple
napi ni yo, not enough, not satisfactory, not sufficient
nazu, to dodge
nazuri, the third
ndaa, booking for, searching for, finding
ndee, to look for, to search for, to find
ndee, winning, defeating, overcoming
Ndere, quiver
ndezu, to win, to defeat, to overcome
ndo, later on, afterwards
ndima, oranges
ndri, goat
ndri ago, a he goat
ndri aroni, a she-goat
ndrii, being handsome, being beauriful, being pretty
ndrizu, to be hansome, to be beautiful, to be pretty
nduu, different
nduuni, a differnt one
nee, seeing, looking at

nezu, to see, to look at
nii , knowing, learning gazing
nii, gazing
nizu, to know, to learn
nizu, to gaze
nore , beads
novemba, november, the 11th month of the year
nyabiliko, scar, mark left by a cured wound
nyadri, grave
nyaka, food
nyaku, soil, ground, the earth
nyali, beads
nyeke, chin
nyoo, breaking
nyondo , hammer
nyozu, to break
nzee, subtracting
nzee, narrating, telling
nzeza , subtraction
nzeza , narrration, tale
nzezu, to subtract
nzezu, to narrate, to tell
nzizaru, heavy
nzila , road
nyamgbiri, red clay
nduale, eastwards
nyampara, foreman
ndu, anus
ndu, buttocks
nyanya, tomatoes
nyiri, tiny, minute
nyiria, tiny ones, small ones
nyure, butter
nyaa, eating, manducating
nyaka, food
nyazu, to eat, to manducate
ngaka, not, yet
ndra drio, long ago

ndri, beauty
nzinzi, spotted
nzetaa, substracting
nguku, back
ngopi ya?, How much? How many?
ndu ndu, differently
ndulu, all
nizaru, ripe
nzizaru, heavy
nzii, squeezing
nzizu, to squeeze
ndia, secretly
ndindiru, silently
ndii ndiiru, truthfully, exactly as expected to be done
ngoa ya?, where?
ngoa?, where?
ngoni?, how?
ngoni ya?, how?
nyoo, breaking
nyozu, to break
nii, getting ripe
nizu, to get ripe
ngoleru, in which direction? towards which place?
napi ni yo, not enough, not sufficient
ngo?, where?
ngoniru, in which manner? how?
ngoo, singing a song
ngozu, to sing a song
ndoyi, name sake

O

O o *is the 15th letter of the Lugbara alphabet*
oaa, starting, living, residing, inhabiting
oaa ayikosi, staying happily
Oaa candisi, staying unhappy
oazu ayikosi, to stay happily
oazu candisi, to stay unhappily
oazu, to stay, t o live, to reside, to inhabit

obapi, Creator, God
obazu, to create
obaliko, a fox, a jackal
obee, tempting, testing, persuading
obelemvu, cheek
oboroje, antelope
obetaa, temptation, test
obezu, to tempt, to test, to persuade
obi, pitcher
obi, behaviour, manner, habit, custom
obi, a crowd, the public, multitude
obi onzi, scandal, bad behaviour
obi onzi fezu, to scandalize
obizu, to winnow
obizu, to catch
obirigo, rhinocerous
obo, a ship, a boat, a canoe, a liner
oboko, the cover that is peeled off, shell
oboloko, a fox, a jackal
obu, a worm
obu, the appropriate season in which white ants are collected for food
obuti, morning,
obuti drio drio, very early in the morning
oce, a dog
oce aroni, a bitch
ocee, keeping, caring for, preserving
ocezu, to keep, to care for, to preserve
ocii, hiding, concealing
ocii, biting, masticating
ocizu, to hide, to conceal
ocizu, to bite, to masticate
ocogo, a dog
ocogo aroni, a bitch
ocogo, misery
odaa, insulting, abusing
odaa, pouring
odazu, to insult, to abuse

odazu, to pour
ode, bait, a worm used for trapping fish
odee, falling
odekele, a newly born baby (Odekua)
odezu, to fall
odii, boxing, giving blows to pounding
odi nyaa,, betraying
odi nyazu, to betray
odorono , a married woman who has deserted her husband for other men
odre , urine
odre suu , urinating
odre suzu, to urinate
odri , mud
odra , bamboo
odriru, muddy
odrukudru , frog, toad
odu , day
odu alu, odu iri, odu na, odu su, odu tau, odu azia, sabiti,
Monday, Tuesday, Wednesday, Thursaday, Friday, Saturday, Sunday
odu , thigh
odu, sleep
odu, oil
odu mokeri, good omen
odu onzirii, bad omen
odu, omen
odu, leopard
odu, a fruit -tree, its fruit (oil)
oduru, oily
odu kozu, to sleep
oduu, setting fire on
oduzu, to set fire on
ofetaa , paying back, fine
ofezu , to pay back
ofi, tsetse fly
ofu, leprosy

ofuba, leper
ofusara, fog, mist,
ofuta , ashes
oga, a tick
ogayi, basket
ogalaku, a piece of stone used for aiming at a target
ogaliri, a flea
ogara , an axe
ogaraba, a European
ogazu, to prevent a person from doing something
ogbee, vomiting
ogbezu, to vomit
ogogo, near
ogu, back-bone
ogu, theft, stealth
oguo, a thief
ogu oguzu, to steal
oh!, an expression of surprise!
ojaa, changing, altering, alteration
ojaa, hatching
ojazu, to change, to alter
ogaa, hatching
ogazu, to hatch
ojazu, to hatch (eggs)
ojii, washing
ojii, carrying here and there
ojio, a representative
ojio , a mediator, a go-between in marriage
ojio, an apostle
ojizu, to wash
ojogo, a witch doctor
ojuruko, red ants
oka, black smith
okalamgba, brown
okalamvu, the end, destiny (factory or an industry)
okaza , rusty, red, hot
okujee, marrying,
oku jezu, to marry

ola, root
olaka, a "y" shaped pole used for opening a granary
olazu, to sleep, to lie down or to put across
ole, cupidity
olezu, to deceive
oleo, a person with such a bad desire or cupidity
olegolegoa, a wizard
oli, wind
oli, egg - plant
oli, scar, a mark left when a wound is cured
olitiria, very small
olokoto, a lizard
olu, tuft
oluzu, to tell
oloto, a wound on a toe usually caused when one stumbles against a stone
olupi, a preacher, a catechist
olurumva, a wound on a toe usually caused when one stumbles against a stone
oma, vagina
ombi, locust
ombizoku, sea, ocean
ombivu, a variety of potato vines
omi, papyrus
ombizoku, ocean, sea, lake
omi, brain
omii, forcing, urging
omiru, brainy, clever, intelligent, brilliant
omizu, to force, to urge
omu, a visitor
omuko, rancour
omuta, banquet
ondre, evening
ondresi, in the evening
ondroko, snore
ondroko soo, snoring
ondroko sozu, to snore
oni, stone, rock, mountain

onitaa, learning
onizu , to learn
onokono , praying mantis
onoo, complaining, murmuring
onozu, to complain, to murmur
omvu, nose
omvusi, mucus
onya , white ants
onyaandri, queen termite
onyofi , finger nails, toe nails
onyoko, food
opaa , a piece of stone or pebble used for throwing at a target. (just a round medium small stone)
paa, robbing,, crucifying, nailing.
opasi, nape
opazu, to rob, to crucify, to nail
ope, guinea fow
opee, sorting out, choosing or selecting
opegu, pig
opendu, favouritism, nepotism
opezu, to sort out, to choose
opi, chief
opi, riches, wealth
opile, waist
opi - le, like a chief or king
opio , a rich man, a wealthy man, a well-to-do man
opi nyaa , ruling,
opi nyazu, to rule
oraa, thinking
orataa, thought, thinking, cogitation
orazu, to think, to cogitate
ori, seed, semen
ori, snake, serpent
ori, fear
ori, louse
oriba, clansmen, people of a clan
orii, rusting
orijo, a place of worship, church, mosque

ori rizu, to sow seeds
orio, fearful
orioru, fearful
orindi, soul of a person that goes to heaven, hell, purgatory or limbo after death
orindi onzi, madness, evil spirit
orizu, to sit down
orizu, to fear
oro, earth, universe, the whole world
orobi, dream
orodri kuru, all over the world
oromi, nine
oru, up, over, on
oru bua, up in the heavens, up in heaven
osaa, slapping
osaa, burying, planting
osaa, mixing
osazu, to slap
osazu, to mix
osazu, to bury, to plant
ose, fat
osee, becoming fat, dragging, pulling
oseru, fat
osezu, to become fat
osezu, to drag, to pull
osii, delivering, giving birth to a child
ositaa, delivery, giving birth, nativity, birth
oso, fats
osofi, lip
osoro, sputum
osolo, sputum
osotaa, convincing a person to do what one wants
osozu, to convince a person to do what you want
osu, beans
osu, bow (figuratively gun)
osuzu, to be surprised
osutaa, mar vel, wonder
osutaaru, marvelous, wonderful

otaa, murmuring, complaining
otazu, to murumur, to complain
otee, waiting
otee, waiting for something or somebody
otee ze, gassing breaking wind
otezu, to wait for
otii, hanging a person
otii, to arrange in order
otii , plucking fruits from a tree
otogo , ant hill (otuko - an ant hill)
otoloo, testicles
otonoko , serpentarius
otu , **navel,** umbillicus
otuu, putting in order
otu, a piece of stone used for throwing at a target
otubi , placenta
otunukua , scorpion
otunyo, white ants left to ferment for a while used as condiment in vegetables
otuo , brother-in-law
otutaa, correction, correcting
otuzu , to correct, to put in order
ovaa , escavating, uprooting
ovazu, to escavate, to uproot
ovii, scratching,
ovizu, to scratch
ovi ni ba sozu, (lightining) striking a person
ovi ni fizu, for the lighting to flash with thunder
ovu , laziness, idleness, indolence
ovuu, staying
ovuzu, to stay
ovolo , over all
owaa , jumping, skipping
owataa, jumping, skipping
owazu, to jump, to skip
owee, sweeping
owezu, to sweep
owii, sacrificing, offering a sacrifice

owii, peeling
owitaa, sacrifice, offering
owizu, to sacrifice, to offer a sacrifice
owizu, to peel
owoko, anger
owokoru, angrily
owuu, crying, weeping, mourning
owuzu, to cry, to weep, to mourn
oyaa, shaking
oyaa, yaws
oyaa, monkey
oyakiya, earth-quake
oyazu , to shake
oyii, to become thin, to thin, to drizzle (ozooni oyizu)
oyizaru, thin
oyizu, to become thin
oyo, promise, vow, oath
oyo soo, promising, vowing, making an oath
oyo sozu, to promise, to vow, to make an oath
oyogo, a monkey
oyoo, a monkey
oyuu, to call shouting
oyuzu, to call by shouting loudly
ozoo, rain
ozoo , roasting
ozoo ni dizu , to rain
ozozu, to roast
ozu, elephant grass
ozuku, porcupine
ozuruko, elephant grass
okurunya, rubbish
obi moke, good manners, virtue
ombe , neck
ongorobi , eyebrow
oliko, throat, voice
obolo , cheek
obelemvu, cheek
ondi, dirt

ondi, sweat, perspiration
otii, brother-in-law
odraa, dying
odrazu, to die
ogua, chair
ondu, sorghum
ombee, leaking
ombezu, to leak
oni andri, grinding stone
ogoa, small axe
okporoa, skin bag
odu dasi, that day
odu diima alea, one of these days
okpo, strength
okpo, a given power, authority
okporu, strong, difficult
ojoo, doctor
ojoo, witch doctor
odika, flue, influenza
opirikele, branch
oduru, a deaf person
okele, cough
okele gaa, coughing
okele gazu, to cough
oro milea, mucus from the eyes
oazu azoro, to be sick, to be ill
oazu edriro, to be healthy, to be alive
oazu abirisi, to be hungry
oazu andezaru, to be tired
oazu eyere, to stay quietly
oazu oriru, to be fearful
oazu orikokoru, to be fearless
omvu coo, sneezing
omvu cozu, to sneeze
obauaua, hyena
oboroje, antelope
odru, buffalo
oku oruu, raping

oku oruzu, to rape
oru, hump
oyu, horn
oje, horn
okuku , tortoise
odu odu, castrated (e.g. a bull or goat)
okondo, ostrich
onyandri, queen termite
ohorokoto, wax without honey
onyukunyu, fly
orodri, reward, prize
obii, imitating
obizu , to imitate
obiru, many, numerous, several
onzoroko , many, numberless
onzivu, ugliness
onzivu ru, ugly
onzi, bad, ugly
onzirikanyaru, very ugly
odi new, fresh
odiru, new, fresh
okporu, hard
okuru, old
oyizaru, thin
odu zuu, everyday, daily
odu dria, everyday, daily
ore, watery
ogogo, near
okpo kokoru, feeble
orule , upwards
ombee, binding, tying
ombezu, to bind, to tie
omvii, answering
omvii, returning
omvizu, to answer
omvizu, to return
omvee, calling
omvezu, to call

obaa, creating
obazu, to create
ongo tuu, dancing
ongo tuzu, to dance
olee, deceiving
olezu, to deceive
ogu, there
omba bazu, to get angry
okuu, gathering
okuzu, to gather
omvee, inviting
omvezu, to invite
obii, measuring
obizu, to measure
ogaa, prohibiting, preventing
ogazu, to prohibit, to prevent
ozoo ni oyizu, to drizzle
omvii, replying
omvizu, to reply
ozii, selling
ozizu, to sell
oraa, flowing
orazu, to flow
obii, trying
obizu, to try
owuu, crying, weeping
owuzu, to cry, to weep
oya, salary, pay, wage

P

P, p *is the 16th letter of the Lugbara alphabet*
pa, leg
paale, times
padiri, a priest
pajama, a pair of pants - (a kiswahili word)
pakasi, servant
paka, up to the extent of (derived from Kiswahili)
pali, a pair of shorts

54

pamba, cotton
panga, punishment, penance
pamvu, foot-print, foot-mark
pa ojii, washing legs
pa ojizu , to wash legs
papa, a child's name for his father
Papa , the Pope, the head of te catholic church on earth
pari, papyrus, papyrus mat
pari, place
pari, a greater part of
pari dri, on papyrus mat
pari ni, a greater part of
parozu, to be saved, to be redeemed
parozu ni yo, no way of escaping
pasi , on foot
pasi, an iron box
pataa, salvation, redemption
pati, tree
patuu, standing
patuzu, to stand
payipayi, pawpaw
pee, selecting, choosing
pere, slasher
pereperea, light
pesa , money (derived from kiswahili)
pilili, nakedness
pi, the whole of it
pililiru, naked
piri , all
piri, straight, upright, erect
piri, at somebody's home e.g. **John piri ,** at John's home
piza, swelling, expansion, increase in size
piza, breadth, the volume
purgotorio, a place where souls of dead people stay for sometime to pay for small sins before they go to heaven
puru , more than required, oversize
purupu ru, doing things without caring
puru, an expression used for a bird flying suddenly
pee, erecting

55

pezu, to erect
putruku, hoof (e.g. of a cow)
pirini, freely, free of charge
pirini, without, freely
pekepeke , light, thin (e.g. of paper)
pari azia, somewhere, elsewhere
pari piria, everywhere
puru puru, carelessness
pikipiki, motorcycle
piripiri, pepper
pii , expanding
pizu, to expand
pii , managing
pizu, to manage
pe (ebi), catching (fish)
pezu, to catch fish
paa, saving, redeeming
paa, hammering, nailing
paa, robbing
pazu, to save
pazu, to redeem
pazu, to rob
piliko, nakedness
paanzi, toes

R

R r *is the 17th letter of the Lugbara alphabet*
raa , thinking, thought
raa , flowing e.g. liquid
rabi, shapeleessly big, clumsy
raka, first
rangi , paint, colour (derived for kiwahili)
rataa, flowing
rataa, thought
ratili, measurement, kilo,
rau, a castrated bull
razu, to flow
razu, to think

re , far
ree , robbing, grabbing
rezu, to rob, to grab
rii, sowing seeds
rizu, to sit
rizu, to sow seeds
robi, hippopotamus
robia , money (derived from rupee, Indian currency)
roo , cursing
rozali, rosary
rozu, to curse
ru Adroo veleri, christian name
ru aparaka veleri, nickname
ru adari, surname
ru daa, naming, giving names e.g to a newly born child
ru dazu, to name, to give names to
ru, name
ro , miss
rudu, bush
ruba , body
rua , body
rumu, name sake
ruu, mating
ruzu, to mate (in animals)
ru, sudden, suddenly
ruu, respecting
ruzu, to respect
ruu, arresting
ruzu , to arrest
rii, court yard, compound
rii, sitting
rizu, to sit
ria ria , peppers
rua atii, recovering from sickness
rua atizu, to recover from sickness
rukusa, permission
raa (enisi), the whole (night) throughout the night.

S

S s *is the 18th letter of the Lugbara alphabet*

saa , planting, burying
saa, watch, clock, hour
saa , at random
saaro, without measure, at random
sabiti, Sunday
sabuni, soap
sadaka, banquet
sambia, acacia tree
sara, not completely full
saturu, a panga
sazu, to plant, to bury
see, dragging, pulling
see, breathing in, inhaling e.g air, smoking
see, flat
sezu, to drag, to pull
sezu, to smoke, to inhale, to breathe in
si? , how many ? How much?
si , teeth
siso, jaw
si , hail stones
sii , writing
sii ,creating, building
sii, worrying, bothering
sinitako, it is not suitable, it is not convinient
siriba , a mulet
sitaa , writing, handwriting
sitani, devil, satan, demon, evil spirit
sitara, it is suitable, it is fit, it is convinient
sizu, to write
sizu, to create, to build
sizu, to worry, to bother
sobi, tail
soka, bed sheets
soo, pricking
soo, sewing clothes

sozu, to prick
sozu, to sew
su, four
su, sap
su, soup
su, diarhoea
suu, wearing
su zu, to wear
sindani, needle
saani, dish
Sabiti, Sunday
sangu, mortar
sangu abe, pestle
saa aro, at 2.00 p.m.
sati, shirt
siya?, How many?
surasura, blue
sero enyia, approaching, coming near somebody
serozu enyia, to approach, to come near somebody
soo, contributing, donating
sozu, to contribute, to donate
saa, slapping
sazu, to slap
sazu (dri), to clap (hands)
saa (dri), clapping (hands)

T

T t *is the 19th letter of the Lugbara alphabet*
ta, food
taa, always, daily
taa, bearing, enduring, tolerating
taba, tobacco
taaza, a lamp
tai, a marvel
tairu, marvelous, miraculous
trotro, spoiling
talakpa, insipid, tasteless
taliru, miraculous, marvelous

tara, a lamp
tokosi, purposely, intentionally
tau, five (5)
tegula, tiles
tala, lamp
tazu, to bear, to endure, to tolerate
te, then
tedi, and then
tee, waiting
teri, load, luggage
tee(ze), breaking wind, gassing
tabasee, smoking
tetaa, waiting
taba sezu, to smoke
tezu, to wait
tezu(ze), to break wind, to gas
ti, a cow
timbilimbi, chin
ti, in vain
ti, language
ti, mouth
tibitibi, beard
tilikpa, tough e.g. uncooked meat
true, almost
ti nzee, speaking a language
ti nzee, mentioning
ti nzezu, to speak a language
ti nzezu, to mention
tiru titi, dressing oneself smartly
tiru titi, hanging oneself, committing suicide
troli, resentment
tiruzu titi, to dress oneself, to commit suicide
toko, zero
tizu, to hang
tibi, vegetables
tizu, to give birth, to deliver, to produce
tibi, beards
toci, torch

toko , without any reason, for nothing
tiko , woven door frame
tokoni, a different one
toli , advice, admonition
turu alu, one hundred (100)
torozi , trousers
too , accusing
totaa , accusation, report
ti pezu , to send on an errand
totaa, filing up a case
totaa , warming up
toto, warm
toko , for nothing
toza , warm
tau , five
tozu, to accuse, to report
tratra , always
tozu, to fill up e.g fill a container
tedi, but
tozu , to warm up
trii, cursing
ti erii, obeying
trii, rubbing, smearing, anointing
tandarua, mosquito net
trizu, to curse
tii erizu, to obey
trizu, to rub to smear, to anoint
ti pee, sending on an errand
tualu, together
turu alo, one hundred
tulu , an axe
turu, bee hive
tusu, saliva
trotro , equal
tusu kii, swallowing saliva
trotrofo!, please!
tusu kizu, to swallow saliva
te , but

tusu wii, spitting
toko , only
tusu wizu, to spit
traitrai, completely
tuu, climbing
tuuni, a different one
tuzu, to climb
tuu bua, going to heaven
tuzu bua , to go to heaven
tii (jo), thatching a house
tii(mva), delivering (a baby)
tii(anzi), producing (children)
tii , dropping (liquids)
tii , hanging
tizu, to deliver
tizu, to produce
tizu, to drop
tizu, to hang
tizu, to thatch a house
tibijo, pot for cooking vegetables
ti kari, a heifer
ti aroni, cow
ti ago, bull

U

U, u *is the 20th letter of the Lugbara alphabet*
uaua, a bird that cries as its name, kookobura
Uara , big
uru , up
uwee, a cry of a baby

V

V, v *is the 21st letter of the Lugbara alphabet*
vaa , guessing
vaa , digging e.g a hole
vaa , down
vaalero , downwards

vaalesi, downwards
vataa , guess
vazu , to guess
vee, burning
velerisi, later on
velesi, later on,
vii, throwing
vii, scratching
vini, and, also, too
vizu, to throw
vizu, to scratch
vo, to e.g. **erivo,** to him, to her, to it
vonavona , soft, comfortable
voro, lung
vuu , (aci), blowing
vuzu (aci), to blow fire
voo, to slash
vu , the universe, world
vi , pus, snot
vii (oli), blowing (wind)
vizu(oli), to blow (e.g. the wind)
vino, ink
vino jo, ink pot, inkwell
vino, wine
vosi siya?, How many times?
vosi alu, once
vosi eri, twice
vosi na, three times, thrice
vutia, behind, during the absence of
vutinia, in the absence of
vaalesi, on the ground
vini endi, also
vini dini le , and also like this

W

W, w *is te 22nd letter of the lugara alphabet*
waa, jumping
waa, proving through risks, even the risk of dying

63

waco, aunt
wadi, relative, wife
wako ko, weak, feeble
wala, large, broad
walala, brown
wara, reeds for weaving a granary
wara, true
wara, shoes
waraga, letter
wari, a poisonous sap of a tree put on the blades of an arrow so that once an animal is shot at, with it, the animal cannot escape death
wazu, to jump
wazu, to prove
wazu, to run away
wee , being handome, being beautiful
wee, sweeping
wee saaro , very handsome, very beautiful
wezu, sweep
wezu, to be beautiful, to be handome
wi, arm
wii, skinning
wiriwiria, sling
wii, spitting
wizi, thread
wizu, to skin
wizu, to spit
woko, part
woro, all
woko, side
woroto, cow dung
woloko ti, arm pit
wudrikuru, all over the world
wu, arm
woko andraleru, southwards
wuu, crying
woko oruleru, northwards

wuzu, to cry
wakili, sub-chief
waa, getting mature
wazu, to get mature
wara, big, great
Wura, colour

Y

Y, y *is the 23rd letter of the LUgbara alphabet*
yaa, winnowing
yaa, shaking, shivering
yaa, sorting
yadi, yard (measurement)
yako, without a mother
yali, cheating
ya, suddenly
yamari, banquet
yaa yee!, an expresion used when expecting danger!
yataa, shaking, shivering
yataa, sorting
yataa, winnowing
yazu, to shake, to shiver
yazu, to sort out
yazu, to winnow
ye, arrow
yebi, spear grass
yee, doing, acting
yefi, bullets (ammunition) - (ye-efi)
ye gbii, shooting with an arrow
ye gbizu, to shoot with an arrow
yeke, o.k. alright, correct, right
yekoko, many, numerous
yekeke, many, numerous
yere, water buck
yeruko, can't be done, impossible
yetaa, doing, action
yezaru, to be done

yezu, to do, to act
yi lemvu, water pot
yi , water
yia , at the site where water can be fetched, In Buganda, crossing the Nile coming to Buganda
yikii, thought, idea
yiru , watery
yi saa, swimming
yi saazu, to swim
yi wee, swimming
yi wezu, to swim
yofe, broom
yo , no, nothing, nil, naught, zero
yoo , talking, saying, speaking, uttering
yozu, to talk, to say, to speak, to utter
yu , poison in a snake
yuku, kite
yuruu , feverish, feeling cold
yiyia , mosquito

Z

Z z *is 24th letter of the Lugbara alphabet*
za , meat
za kalanya , beef
zamva, a girl
ze, faeces, waste matter, dung (shit) excrement
ze otezu, to break wind
zee , defecating
zee , pushing
zezu, to push
zero, zero
ze tee, breaking wind, gassing
ze tezu, to break wind, to gas
ze zee, defecating, excreting, emptying the bowels
ze zezu , to defecate, to excrete, to empty one's bowels,
zii , daughter

zii, questioning, asking
zii, greeting
zii, opening
zii, to hide, to conceal
zirozaru, questionable/ **zirozaru** = hidden, concealed
zirozu, to hide, to conceal
zizu, to question
zizu, to greet
zizu , to open
zizu , to hide
zoo, crossing e.g. a river
zoo, milking e.g. a cow
zoo, growing
zuu (ayiko), rejoicing, making merry, carousing
zotaa, growth
zoza , the length
zoza , growth
zozo, far, distant, lengthy, long
zozu, to grow
zozu, to milk
zuzu (ayiko), to rejoice, to make merry, to carouse
zuu, always, daily

Useful Phrases

English
Lugbara

1. What do you want?
   I Ie a'do ya?
2. I do not understand what you say.
   Ma eri e'yo mini 'yoleri ko.
3. Repeat it please.
   I'yo dika fo.
4. Where do you come from?
   Mi ebi nga ngoa ya?
5. Where are you going?
   Mi mungoa ya?
6. Do you understand English?
   Mi English ti erira ya?
7. I can not speak English.
   A ni Inglisi ti ko.
8. Sweep this room well.
   I we jo 'di ma ale moke.
9. Are you ready?
   Mi ngonde ya?
10. I am very glad to see you.
    A wadifoo mani mi ne le si.
11. Follow this road.
    I bi geri 'diri.
12. At what time shall I come?
    Ma nga emu saa si a ?
13. Is your master at home?
    Ambo miveleri akua?
14. He is not here.
    Eri 'doa yo.
15. May I come in?
    Ma eco fizo ra?
16. Come in.
    Mi efi.
17. Wait a moment.
    I te nga were.

18. I do not know.
    Ani ko.
19. I do not want it.
    A le ko.
20. I do not believe it.
    Ma a'i ko.
21. What time is it?
    Saa ca si a?
22. Very well.
    Moke to.
23. Come here.
    Mi emu 'doa.

Proverbs, Idioms and Similes

1. **Abazu koro**, to be dumbfounded
2. **Eyo adari luzu hu,** to tell the plain truth
3. **Adrizu dri ondi be**, to be a poisoner
4. **Adrizu ndrizaru eri anyani**, to be handsome or beautiful, first, one has to feed well.
5. **Adrizu dri be ezu**, to be a thief
6. **Ocogo ni ama ari mbezu mibe**, to fight to a man
7. **Eyo ni ndrizu abua le,** to iron differences, not to revenge
8. **Yozu maye dere bile apibo**, to weep over spilt milk
9. **Ba bizu kporokporo**, to catch red handed
10. **Yozu otuo ma azici te adro ma azi yo**, to prefer the existence of an uncle to that of a brother-in-law, if one marries another woman one can always have another brother-in-law but not another uncle.
11. **Dri alu ni azi ngazu ko**, to have two heads in decision taking
12. **Adrizu ovuo nyazu ku,** to work in order to obtain one's living
13. **Edri ni ovuzu nyani**, to eat in order to live
14. **Ka ayira boro mapa liri**, he will categorically say 'no'
15. **Aparaka ma tibi agobi**, frivolity is bad

16. **Mile aci nyani, riri nyani,** curiousity kills a cat
17. **Asi nyani,** perseverance pays
18. **Asiteza nyani,** patience pays
19. **Bile api bo,** it is too late
20. **Orio nyani,** cowards live longer
21. **Eyere nyani,** patience pays
22. **Adi endu oree,** Proverbs
23. **Azavuo mamva ni aku bani,** The son of a filthy and disregarded person builds a home
24. **Okuku dra drinza si oboa ,** inferiority complex is bad
25. **Drinza nya modo,** a shy person gets the least portion of a thing, e.g. meat
26. **Abiri ma eli ciku** , Hunger does not kill in an instant
27. **Edroo nya angu owu matiaku,** Everyday has its happenings
28. **Anyisi adamanaka ve acia,** pride is bad
29. **Eriku dri ai ca tibi a ku,** misunderstanding causes a lot of inconviniences
30. **Eba ma anyaru beni ma awuzi ru ya?,** Why do you keep mistreating me like this? e.g. a house wife.
31. **Do kani obi acoro nika,** At a child's death people say, even if it dies, there shouldn't be much worry, so long the surviving parents are alive, they will have another baby, God willing.
32. **Mini ri miniaa,** Do not tamper with one's relatives well being. Blood is thicker than water, nduvunduvu.
33. **Ti kari ni onii nva ivele okorisi,** Experience is the best teacher.
34. **Emvu ni i acoo katia ,** misfortune comes in when one is about to succeed in an ordeal
35. **Yoni ma akosi Egania fi okporo vu,** necessity has no law
36. **Bama endu ndazu,** to undermine a person.
37. **Afusi ndalaka ve lemiko a,** pride is bad
38. **Vulevule mvu eji , vulevule gbi endiria,** a late comer gets the least

39. **Drinza nya onde**, a shy person gets the worst part of a thing
40. **Kpakpa nze fa**, it is not wise to do things in a hurry
41. **Opasi ma drinzayo,** what happens during one's absence does not affect one
42. **Anyama tibi go osupi ku** , a very small piece of meat is enough for eating a big quantity of posho
43. **Asi eri oceni, te mile eri libanda ni,** What is in the heart is not known but what is on the face is clear

www.ingramcontent.com/pod-product-compliance
Lightning Source LLC
Chambersburg PA
CBHW070741230426
43669CB00014B/2541